P is for Palmetto

A South Carolina Alphabet

Written by Carol Crane and Illustrated by Mary Whyte

Sleeping Bear Press™

2395 South Huron Parkway, Suite 200
Ann Arbor, MI 48104
www.sleepingbearpress.com

Printed and bound in the United States.

19 18 17

Library of Congress Cataloging-in-Publication Data

Crane, Carol, 1933-
P is for palmetto : a South Carolina alphabet / by Carol Crane;
illustrated by Mary Whyte.
p. cm.
Summary: Presents information about the state of South Carolina in an
alphabetical arrangement.
ISBN 978-1-58536-047-5
1. South Carolina—Juvenile literature. 2. English
language—Alphabet—Juvenile literature. [1. South Carolina. 2.
Alphabet.] I. Whyte, Mary, ill. II. Title.
F269.3 .C73 2002
975.7—dc21   2002004301

To Howard and Fran Ward,
life-long residents of Pawleys Island,
and to Diane and Morgan Crane.

CAROL

For Rachel Hodges,
a great First Lady of South Carolina,
in appreciation for her role as ambassador
of reading in the state.

MARY

A a

Once you have seen the Angel oak tree, you will never forget this awesome sight. The tree shades an area of 17,000 square feet with enormous limbs that touch the ground and then head right for the sky. This magnificent live oak tree is considered to be over 1,400 years old and is the oldest living thing east of the Mississippi River. The tree gets its name from the Angel family who once owned the land on which it grows. This tree is found on Johns Island, south of Charleston.

A is for the Angel oak tree,
    massive limbs greeting the sky.
    I wish it could tell me the stories,
of years it has seen pass by.

During plantation days, large work baskets were used for collecting and storing rice, grain, cotton, fish, and shellfish. The large baskets were woven of bulrush. Vegetables, fruits, and bread were stored in sweetgrass baskets made for home use. Basket making involved the whole family. Men and boys gathered the materials, while women and girls wove the baskets. Long hours of work are involved in making the baskets. Some of the designs take two or three months to weave. The grasses used in the baskets are from wetlands and marsh areas in the lowcountry. This type of basketry is one of the oldest crafts of African origin in America.

B is for sweetgrass Baskets,
    a rich history of African-American art.
Woven by families for 300 years,
    a heritage that comes from the heart.

C c

Now **C** is for Columbia,
the capital of our state.
Here the rules and laws are made
that make our state so great!

Columbia is located in the center of South Carolina. It was named after Christopher Columbus. Columbia was laid out by the legislature in 1786 as the new state capital. All of the rules and laws of our state are made and voted on by our representatives, senators, and our governor. The statehouse has some of the largest columns in the world. Each column stands 43 feet high, weighs 37 tons and has been cut from a single piece of stone.

Drayton Hall is the only plantation house on the Ashley River to survive the Revolutionary War and the Civil War unchanged. After two wars, hurricanes, earthquakes, and seven generations of the John Drayton family, the house remains in nearly original condition. The house has no running water, electric lighting, or central heating. Just think: no television, no refrigerator, or heat during those cold winter nights!

D is for Drayton Hall,
    a majestic southern plantation.
Built on the Ashley River in 1742,
one of the oldest in our nation.

South Carolina designated the eastern tiger swallowtail as the official butterfly of the state. It is of particular interest to gardeners and farmers with orchards, as the butterfly is a great pollinator. It can be seen throughout South Carolina along streams, rivers, wooded swamps, and in towns and cities.

E is for the Eastern tiger swallowtail,
a colorful butterfly to see.
Flying from flower to flower,
flitting and soaring, wild and carefree.

Francis Marion fought the British during the Revolutionary War. As a captain, he formed a company of men to fight for freedom by fighting the British in small surprise attacks. This company of men, who became known as "Marion's Men," would set up their camps in the swamps of South Carolina where the British could not find them. In 1936, our state honored Francis Marion by naming 250,000 acres of land the Francis Marion National Forest.

The swamps that Francis Marion took shelter in are a wonderful part of South Carolina. The Congaree Swamp National Monument has very tall loblolly pine trees—some are 300 years old and 145 feet tall. This swamp is also home to the bald cypress tree, which has knees (or roots) that grow from the root system to well above the average water level. Flooding occurs at least ten times a year and leaves deposits of rich soil. The swamp has some of the tallest trees in the east, which form one of the highest canopies (or roofs) in the world, making a perfect home for woodpeckers, bobcats, owls, deer, and other wildlife including snakes and skinks.

Ff

Now F is for the Swamp Fox.
Francis Marion was his true name.
A hero of the Revolutionary War,
a Carolinian of great fame.

G stands for the Grand Strand—
cool ocean breezes, sun, and sand.
Fishing piers stretching out into the ocean,
families walking hand in hand.

The Grand Strand (meaning shore) is on the Atlantic Ocean. For 60 miles, it includes all the shoreline from Winyah Bay and Georgetown, northeast to Little River Neck on the North Carolina state line. Pawleys Island, the oldest resort beach in South Carolina and possibly the U.S., Murrells Inlet, Litchfield Beach, and Myrtle Beach are some of the places vacationers go to swim, hunt for shells, fish, and enjoy the beautiful seashore. The Intracoastal Waterway is west of the Grand Strand. This is a water road that boats use to travel safely from north to south or south to north, instead of the large ocean. The salt marshes are also an important part of the coastal plains.

The horse has been an important part of South Carolina's story. From plowing fields, to hunting, racing, jumping, and pleasure riding, this valiant steed has been part of the scenery. The many horse lovers of our state are found riding through the ocean surf at dawn, riding the mountain trails, or watching the training of race horses in Aiken and Camden, S.C. The Thoroughbred Hall of Fame is found in Aiken, S.C.

h

H

H is for Horse,
    faithful throughout our history.
Most beautiful and noble beast,
    our love for you is no mystery.

Indigo is a rich, purple-blue dye first grown in India. It is a difficult plant to grow and plantation owners hoped to find some place in America where it would grow. Europe does not have a favorable climate for growing indigo, which is a difficult plant to grow. Colonel George Lucas sent his daughter, Eliza Lucas Pinckney, some indigo plants to test the soil of the plantation she ran for him near Charleston. The plants were killed by a frost the first year and insects ate the plants the second year, but Eliza was successful the third year and grew a large crop of indigo. By not giving up, Eliza's plantation and others in South Carolina became known as the best place to grow indigo in the world. The entire indigo plant is cultivated and processed until the dye is in powder form, then that powder is used to color material.

I i

The Indigo plant is our letter I,
it makes a dye so royal to see.
A valuable crop for plantations,
first grown in 1743.

J j

J stands for James Island
where, at the start of the Civil War,
the first shot was fired,
written in history evermore.

The Civil War started when Forts Johnson and Moultrie fired on Fort Sumter after the Union army refused to withdraw from the fort. After 34 hours of bombardment by the cannons from James Island and Sullivan's Island, the Union officer and his men withdrew. Fort Sumter is located in the middle of Charleston Harbor on a manmade island. It has been made into a National Historical Site. Forts Johnson and Moultrie were on either side of the main shipping channel that led to the city of Charleston. Many brave Confederate soldiers fought to save their main harbor and city.

K is for King Cotton,
blossoms from pink to fluffy white.
Grown for years in the fields,
harvesters working day and night.

Cotton has been "King" in South Carolina for hundreds of years. From the field to fabric, this plant has provided us with cotton pants, jeans, shirts, socks, and many more clothing items. The lint from cotton is put into dollar bills along with another fabric, linen. So "paper" money is really made from cotton! The seed from the cotton plant is squeezed and an oil is refined to be used in cooking. This oil also makes margarine, lard, and soap. Santee Cooper Country is the state's top cotton producing area.

k

K

L is for the Loggerhead sea turtle,
our state's three-hundred-pound reptile.
Nesting along our coast,
swimming and feeding, mile after mile.

The loggerhead sea turtle is one of South Carolina's state symbols. This large reddish brown turtle likes the warm waters off the coast of our state. It has a jaw more powerful for its size than an alligator's. They use these powerful jaws to eat hard-shelled animals such as crabs and clams. They are very powerful yet graceful swimmers as their flippers are used like paddles. These majestic sea turtles are protected by our government.

Ll

Mary McLeod Bethune spent her 80 years working, educating, and advising four presidents. After teaching for many years, she founded and became president of the Bethune-Cookman College in Daytona Beach, Florida. She was an advisor to President Franklin D. Roosevelt, and was the first African-American woman to head a federal agency.

m

M

M stands for Mayesville and also Mary—
Mary McLeod Bethune was born here.
Education for all of our people
was her goal and lifelong career.

This wildlife refuge is home to many species of waterfowl that spend the winters here in this warm climate. The Santee National Wildlife Refuge was established in 1941 and is located in the upper coastal plains of South Carolina. This area is perfect for many types of birds as it has ponds, open waters, hardwood and pine trees, and marshes. It is fun to count how many types of birds you can see! People who track the birds and watch them give them codes such as "permanent resident," "winter visitor," "summer resident," "transient" (which means comes and goes), and "accidental" (which means they flew in to see what is going on).

The Santee Cooper Lake system has two great fishing lakes, Lake Marion and Lake Moultrie. South Carolina's state fish, the striped bass, is the state's most famous game fish. Many record-sized fish have been caught in this area.

n
N

N stands for the National Wildlife Refuge at Santee,
where in fall, Canada geese arrive.
They land on the waters of Lake Marion,
and I love to hear them honk, splash, and dive.

Oo

Along the banks of the Savannah River, Native Americans some 4,500 years ago discovered that fire could harden clay to a stone-like form. These unknown people mixed Spanish moss or palmetto fibers with the clay to make the earliest known pottery vessels in North America.

Back in the 1800s there were no department stores to buy kitchen containers such as jars, pitchers, and bowls. The Edgefield area is rich in clay and a pottery tradition began based on this work of the early people of South Carolina. These pottery vessels were used for storage of food, water and vinegar. Marbles, for the children to play with, were also made from the clay.

You can visit Old Edgefield Pottery in Edgefield today to see demonstrations and lectures on the history of this fascinating pottery tradition!

O is for Old Edgefield Pottery,
made from South Carolina clay.
Bowls, dishes, and water jugs,
kitchenware used every day.

P is for Palmetto,
our official state tree.
It's also a symbol on our flag,
respected by you and me.

The palmetto tree is also called the sabal or cabbage palm. The trees played an important part in the Revolutionary War. Fort Moultrie, on Sullivan's Island, was made of palmetto logs as a seacoast defense against the British. The fort withstood British attack.

Colonel William Moultrie was asked by the Revolutionary Council of Safety to design a flag. He chose a blue that matched the color of the soldier's uniforms and the crescent that was a silver emblem worn on the front of their caps. A palmetto tree was added to Moultrie's original design. South Carolina has honored the palmetto tree by naming it the state tree. The official state flag was created on January 28, 1861. The crescent and palmetto palm flag flies proudly over the state today.

Blackbeard the pirate was a fierce looking man with a long, black beard. He looked for ships to plunder that were slow and heavy with treasure. In May, 1718, Blackbeard and his men captured and held several rich travelers near Charleston. He sent a boat to the Charleston shore with demands for medicine for his men, not gold or silver. Blackbeard stopped any boats coming into or out of Charleston Harbor for one week. This was called a blockade. He let the hostages go and sailed away to hide in the many coves along the Carolina shore.

Q q

Q stands for *Queen Anne's Revenge,*
    a ship lurking along the coast.
        Blackbeard the pirate seeking treasure,
    in and out of the fog like a ghost.

These attached homes, built in the mid-18th century, have endured the tests of time. Built by merchants who did business on the first floor and lived with their families on the second floor, these houses were ideally located on Charleston's busy seaport. Through time, a devastating fire burned most of Charleston's waterfront, an earthquake shook the city, and four hurricanes ravaged the area. These buildings were restored in the 1930s and painted in bright pastel colors, earning this collection of historic homes the nickname "Rainbow Row." Today there are 14 surviving homes owned and beautifully kept by private owners.

R is for Rainbow Row,
a color wheel of houses.
Through history, time, and fire,
they stand for us to admire.

S is for the Sculpture Gardens,
small and large figurines so alive.
Brookgreen Gardens is the home
where art, flowers, and nature do thrive.

Archer Milton Huntington and his
wife Anna Hyatt Huntington bought
Brookgreen Plantation along with
other lowcountry plantations in 1930.
Together, they set about to fill the area
with breathtaking gardens, a wildlife
trail, and a wonderful sculpture collection for everyone to enjoy. Once a rice
plantation, it is now a place full of
wonder, beauty, and history.

Polly put the kettle on,
we'll all have tea.
South Carolina's favorite drink
Tea begins with T.

Tt

Iced or hot tea is the favorite hospitality drink of South Carolina. The English brought the custom of afternoon tea to America. To this day, little girls have favorite toy tea sets and serve tea and cookies to their friends. The first commercial tea farm in the United States was in Summerville, S.C. Today, the nation's only commercial tea farm is located on Wadmalaw Island, near Charleston, S.C. Even with this rich history of tea in South Carolina, milk is the official state beverage!

Now, U stands for Upcountry,
with panoramic views.
Mountains and waterfalls,
sunsets of vivid hues.

Upcountry is peach and apple growing country. Old grist mills, still in operation, grind cornmeal, flour, and grits. There are also textile mills, a large part of South Carolina's economy. The Chattooga, one of the longest, largest, and most undeveloped free-flowing mountain rivers, has been named one of the best whitewater rafting rivers in North America.

The Cherokee Indians were once a major presence in Upper South Carolina. Many Cherokee legends are told about area landmarks. Table Rock Mountain is said to be the table of a giant Indian chief. Sassafras Mountain at 3,554 feet is the highest point in South Carolina where four states can be seen: Tennessee, North Carolina, South Carolina, and Georgia. This region is the home of many rare, endangered plant and animal species.

V stands for Venus's-flytrap.
Watch out, little bug, don't be trapped!
If you touch the trigger hairs,
the sweet-baited snare will be snapped.

The Venus's-flytrap is a carnivorous plant that feeds on insects and other small animals. It is a native plant found in the northeast coastal plains of South Carolina's savannahs and bogs. It has small white flowers. The leaves are divided into two halves and are the traps. They have a sweet odor that attracts insects and when the trigger hairs are touched, the leaves snap shut. The insect is trapped by the plant's sticky substance. It can take up to ten days for the plant's acidic juices to digest its victim. The plant then opens up its snare again to lure its next victim.

W is for the Carolina Wren,
a sassy, quick little bird.
Singing *tea-ket-tle*, *tea-ket-tle*,
day and night, it can be heard.

The Carolina wren is the official state bird. When nesting, it will make a feather-lined, domed stick nest with an entrance on the side. It likes to make nests in stone walls, hollow tree stumps, tin cans, mail boxes, birdhouses, and even coat pockets on a clothesline. Darting and flitting about, it is seen in all parts of the state.

W
W

The *H.L. Hunley*, a submarine created by Confederate engineers, was discovered on the bottom of Charleston Harbor in 1995. This ironclad Civil War vessel had been lying undetected for over 130 years. This great finding has given a renewed glory to the men who served in this Civil War submarine. These men loved their country and their families and South Carolina respects their courageous deeds.

X marks the spot in history,
in Charleston Harbor on the ocean floor,
where a deep mystery was uncovered—
the *H.L. Hunley* lying, since 1864.

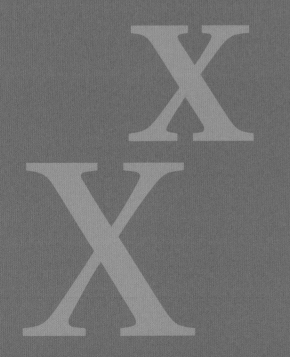

Y y

Y is for Yellow jessamine,
a sweet fragrance that fills the air.
We know that spring is here,
gold flowers are everywhere!

The state flower of South Carolina is the yellow jessamine, also called yellow jasmine. When walking in the woods, you may see these inch-long, trumpet-shaped blossoms on the ground. The vines may also climb fence posts or trees, forever looking for the sun.

The Riverbanks Zoological Park and Botanical Garden in Columbia is rated one of the 10 best zoos in the country. Instead of bars and cages, more than 2,000 animals live in a naturalistic setting created by making use of water and moat barriers. There is also an aquarium, a reptile complex, birdhouse, and daily milking demonstrations at the interactive farm where cows and other farm animals live. A 70-acre botanical garden with woodlands, gardens, and plant collections can be enjoyed in this beautiful place where conservation of flora and fauna is practiced.

Z z

With woodlands, gardens, and historic ruins,
ewes, bears, lions, and a kangaroo.
Z Between the Broad and Saluda rivers,
stands for the Riverbanks Zoo.

A Path Full of Facts

1. Pawleys Island is famous for producing what form of bed?

2. What building served as a dungeon in Charleston?

3. The Boykin Spaniel, the state dog of South Carolina, is known for what?

4. What famous Indian Chief died and is buried in the prison at Fort Moultrie?

5. What was the name of the ship that landed the first settlers in 1670?

6. What two rivers are on either side of Charleston?

7. The first lighthouse, built as early as 1795, burned what oil?

8. South Carolina is divided up into three major regions. What are they?

9. What insect ruined the cotton plants?

10. Many Native American families with sing-song names lived in South Carolina. What is the translated name for Pee Dee? Wee Nee?

11. What plant gave Georgetown County its first economic wealth? What crops were second and third?

12. What was "Waccamaw Gold" from Carolina?

13. What was called the "The Best Friend of Charleston?"

14. Why was Edgar Allan Poe at Fort Moultrie?

15. Who was the first U.S. Senator elected by a write-in vote?

16. South Carolina has two mottos. What are they?

17. What is the emblem of authority for the state's House of Representatives?

18. President Woodrow Wilson's boyhood home is located in what city?

19. What is one of the longest blackwater rivers in the world?

20. What is the name of the state insect of South Carolina?

21. The shag is the official dance of South Carolina. What type of music is used to dance to this music?

22. Along the South Carolina coast, we find the official state shell of this state. What is it?

23. What famous general visited Charleston in 1791?

24. Ninety Six National Historic Site is named for what?

Reference List

Fox, William Price. 1998. *South Carolina: Off the Beaten Path*. Old Saybrook, Connecticut: The Globe Pequot Press.

Jordan, Laylon Wayne and Stringfellow, Elizabeth H. 2000. *A Place Called St. John's*. Spartanburg, South Carolina: The Reprint Company, Publishers.

Meyer, Peter. 1998. *Nature Guide to the Carolina Coast*. Wilmington, North Carolina: Aviav-Cetacean Press.

Phillips, G. Robert. 1992. *Historical Highlights of Charleston*. Charleston, South Carolina: P & R Enterprises.

Thurmond, Gwen, ed. 2000. *South Carolina Smiles*. Columbia, South Carolina.

———. 2000. *South Carolina Places*. Columbia, South Carolina: South Carolina Department of Parks, Recreation, and Tourism.

Todd, Caroline and Wait, Sidney. 1998. *South Carolina a Day at a Time*. Orangeburg, South Carolina: Sandlapper Publishing Company, Inc.

Answers

1. Pawleys Island Hammocks were first created by riverboat captain Joshua John Ward in 1889. He designed a bed made from cotton that was comfortable and cool.

2. The Old Exchange and Provost Dungeon.

3. "The dog that doesn't rock the boat."

4. Osceola.

5. The *Carolina*.

6. The Ashley and the Cooper.

7. Whale oil was burned. The light on the North Island Lighthouse on Winyah Bay is 85 ft. tall and is the last manually operated lighthouse. It can only be reached by boat.

8. The Blue Ridge Mountains, the Piedmont Plateau, and the Atlantic Coastal Plain.

9. The boll weevil.

10. Pee Dee means coming and going and Wee Nee means blackwater or dark water people.

11. The first crop was rice, the second was indigo, and the third was cotton.

12. The long golden grain rice grown in Georgetown County.

13. The South Carolina Canal & Railroad Company began running the nation's first railroad. The first engine was named "The Best Friend of Charleston."

14. Poe's battery was transferred to Fort Moultrie. While on Sullivan's Island he wrote the poem *Al Aaraaf* and the story *The Gold-Bug*.

15. Strom Thurmond, November 2, 1954.

16. "While I Breathe, I Hope" and "Prepared in Mind and Resources."

17. The Mace. The Sergeant-at-Arms walks ahead of the Speaker and lays the Mace on a special rack on the rostrum. The Mace was made in London, in 1756.

18. Columbia.

19. The Edisto River.

20. The Carolina mantid, or praying mantis. This insect plays an important role in helping to control harmful insects.

21. Rhythm and blues.

22. The lettered olive.

23. General George Washington.

24. The unusual name given to a fort by the early traders in the 1700's. They mistakenly believed it was the estimated number of miles from the fort to the Cherokee village of Keowee in the upper South Carolina foothills.

Carol Crane

Lecturer and book reviewer Carol Crane is widely recognized by many schools and educators for her expertise in children's literature. She has conducted in-service seminars for teachers at many schools across the country. Eight years ago Carol instituted a summer reading program for teachers and media specialists.

P is for Palmetto is Carol's latest book with Sleeping Bear Press. She has also authored *P is for Peach: A Georgia Alphabet*; *L is for Last Frontier: An Alaska Alphabet*; *L is for Lone Star: A Texas Alphabet*; *Sunny Numbers: A Florida Counting Book,* and *S is for Sunshine: A Florida Alphabet*. She travels extensively speaking at state reading conventions across the United States and lives in Michigan, Florida, and North Carolina.

Mary Whyte

Mary Whyte has earned national recognition as both an artist and illustrator, exhibiting in such prestigious shows as the American Watercolor Society and the Allied Artists of America. Perhaps best known for her distinctive portraits, Whyte has traveled the country capturing personalities on canvas and paper. Whether of a child in a tree or a judge in official robes, Whyte's portraits grace hundreds of private homes, universities, and corporate collections.

She is a graduate of the Tyler School of Art in Philadelphia, PA. and conducts painting workshops across the country. She and her husband Smith Coleman own an art gallery in Charleston, S.C., near where they live.